CW01370838

The Acharnians of Aristophanes

You are holding a reproduction of an original work that is in the public domain in the United States of America, and possibly other countries.You may freely copy and distribute this work as no entity (individual or corporate) has a copyright on the body of the work.This book may contain prior copyright references, and library stamps (as most of these works were scanned from library copies).These have been scanned and retained as part of the historical artifact.

This book may have occasional imperfections such as missing or blurred pages, poor pictures, errant marks, etc. that were either part of the original artifact, or were introduced by the scanning process. We believe this work is culturally important, and despite the imperfections, have elected to bring it back into print as part of our continuing commitment to the preservation of printed works worldwide. We appreciate your understanding of the imperfections in the preservation process, and hope you enjoy this valuable book.

THE ACHARNIANS

OF

ARISTOPHANES

TRANSLATED INTO ENGLISH VERSE
BY
CHARLES JAMES BILLSON, B.A.
CORPUS CHRISTI COLLEGE, OXFORD

LONDON
KEGAN PAUL, TRENCH & CO., 1, PATERNOSTER SQUARE
1882

PREFACE.

In the following translation I have attempted to present "The Acharnians" to English readers in the spirit of a lively acting play. With this aim in view, I have rendered the dialogue throughout in the free rhyming metre of modern burlesque, which does not even shrink, upon occasion, from a bad rhyme. It has been the usual practice of translators to represent the Greek iambic metre in English by blank verse; and there is certainly no finer mode of expressing the ordered march of the tragic rhythm. But for the less restrained comic iambic, the loose unrhymed verse generally adopted seems but a poor substitute, giving no adequate compensation for the lost point and emphasis of the original. This point and emphasis I have endeavoured, with scant success, to preserve.

English readers must not, of course, take this version to be, even in attempt, Aristophanic. The soul of Aristophanes "dwelleth not in a dry place," and his audacious Bacchic licence is out of date in the "cool shades of modern Protestantism." Some passages in this play have been thus necessarily omitted, and others (*e.g.* the Phallic Hymn) have been, as the only alternative to their omission, hopelessly modernized.

The notes are purely explanatory and illustrative, and do not touch upon any points of scholarship.

INTRODUCTION.

THE oldest comedy that has come down to modern times is that which Aristophanes produced at Athens in the spring of the year B.C. 425. It has, moreover, the less fictitious interest of being one of the best plays that were ever written. "The Acharnians" was a bold but good-natured attack upon the Athenian "Jingoes," who combined a bitter hatred of Sparta with an intense desire for the aggrandizement of "imperial" Athens. The critical instinct of great satirists usually inclines them to side with the minority; but Aristophanes had strong and solid reasons for his view of the situation, which might have convinced the most practical statesman. The Peloponnesian war had lasted five years, and the Athenians, reduced by the ravages of their enemies, and still more by the terrible visitation of the plague, had shown an elasticity under sufferings almost unparalleled in history. Their pride, so far from "falling with their fortunes," rose higher at every reverse, and shrank from making overtures of peace to the exulting Spartan. This sanguine buoyancy of disposition prepared those who knew Athens best for the astounding levity which afterwards marked her conduct: but while there were many who saw no hope for their fellow-countrymen, if they strayed too far from the old and well-tried paths, and who distrusted their airy visions and perpetual childish longing for "some new thing;" yet these were, for the most part, like "poor relenting Nicias," unable to stem the tide of popular enthusiasm, and either turned it to their personal advantage, or were swept away to their destruction. Aristophanes, however, under the mask of comedy, did not hesitate to oppose, with all his powers of ridicule and invective, the fatal delusion of the people. It is in this play that he first speaks out boldly in favour of peace, and the apologetic, though firm, tone which he assumes shows the risk which he ran. His apprehensions were not realized, for the volatile Athenians, always ready to enjoy a joke at their own expense, only laughed good-humouredly, and gave him the first prize. They were content to kiss the rod, without profiting by its correction.

The Acharnians are well chosen to represent the most bitter zealots of the war. Their fertile and populous suburb, which lay about eight miles from Athens, was desolated year after year by the invasions of Sparta; and their military character is evidenced by the fact that at the commencement of the war they furnished a tenth of the whole regular infantry.

The scene of the play is laid on the Pnyx, the meeting-place of the "ecclesia," or public assembly of the citizens. The "Pnyx" lay to the west of the Areiopagus, on a slope connected with Mount Lycabettus. A semicircular space, with an area of about twelve thousand square yards, was marked out upon the side of the hill, and levelled by means of large stones built up to a sufficient height from the lower ground. Here stood the *bema*, a platform cut out of the solid rock, from which the Attic orators spoke, in full view of the Parthenon and all the eloquent monuments of Athenian greatness.

The public assemblies which met upon the Pnyx were summoned and presided over by the members of the Senate of Five Hundred, who were called Prytanies, and one of whose number was appointed chairman every day in the week.

At the opening of the play Dicæopolis (whose name means "good citizen"), the hero of the piece, who represents throughout the views of Aristophanes, is discovered sitting in the Pnyx, and waiting for the citizens to assemble. He is very much disgusted with his lot, and, casting up his accounts, shows that the pleasures and pains are very unfairly balanced. *Item*, to seeing Cleon, the notorious demagogue, prosecuted; 1, "pure poetic pleasure:" *Item*, to hearing Theognis instead of Æschylus in the theatre, 1, "tragical disappointment," etc. The times are altogether out of joint, and he resolves to set them right by a policy of obstruction. Just as he arrives at this determination, the light-hearted crowd of Athenian citizens comes pouring in, "like troutlets in a stream," to deliberate upon affairs of State. The Herald makes proclamation, "Who wishes to harangue?" whereupon an insignificant little personage gets on his legs and declares that he has a special mission from the gods to make a peace, upon which he is promptly removed by the police. The assembly then listens to the travellers' tales of some ambassadors, who excite the wrath of Dicæopolis, and he sends Amphitheüs to Sparta to make a private peace for himself and his family. His messenger soon returns, running violently, for he is being pursued and stoned by some old Acharnian fire-eaters, who will have nothing to do with peaces. However, he has brought Dicæopolis three samples of truces, from which that worthy selects one for thirty years, and retires to his house to celebrate the Feast of Bacchus. After he has marched in solemn procession round the stage with his daughter and maid-servant, he is set upon by the Chorus of old Acharnians, with whom he has to endeavour to justify himself for concluding the peace. He contends that the Spartans are not so black as they are painted, and, when this argument only enrages his hearers the more, has resource to a stratagem, and so obtains leave to make them a speech upon the subject with his head upon a chopping-block. But first he deems it prudent to borrow an appropriate tragedy costume from Euripides, the new-fangled poet of common life. Having obtained this, he comes out and speaks for his life, with such effect that he wins over to his cause one half of the Chorus. The other half, however, still clamour for war, and call in Lamachus, the great general. When that hero appears upon the scene, he immediately becomes a butt for the ridicule of Dicæopolis, who abuses him soundly, first for his military appearance and spirit, and then as representative of those young ambassadors who, through favouritism, were continually being sent off to Thrace and Sicily and all kinds of ridiculous places, doing no work, but drawing a high salary.

Tried veterans, like these old Acharnians, he complains, never get these sinecures. Upon hearing this, Lamachus expresses his resolution of waging war with Sparta to the death, and Dicæopolis proclaims that he is about to open a market for the use of the Lacedæmonians and their allies, and the Megarians and Bœotians; in fact, for the use of all the world—except Lamachus.

Here follows the Parabasis, in which the poet, through the mouth of the Chorus, answers the charge of libelling the State which had been brought against him. After an invocation to the Muse in lyric verse, the Chorus goes on to complain of the ingratitude shown by the State to her old servants, and of the scandalous way in which they are brow-beaten in the law courts by ready-tongued and profligate young barristers.

Meantime the news of Dicæopolis's open market has travelled far, and the first person to arrive is a Megarian, accompanied by two little daughters. The Athenian market-place, from which they were excluded by a special decree, is a delightful spot to men of his country. However, he is so poor that he has nothing to sell or exchange, until the expedient suggests itself to him of selling his two daughters in sacks as little pigs. He thus disposes of them to Dicæopolis for some salt and garlic, and, thanks to Dicæopolis's cat-o'-nine-tails, escapes from an intrusive informer. The Chorus now sing some verses congratulating Dicæopolis upon the success of his peace. The next person who comes to market is a Bœotian, who arrives accompanied by a boy laden with all kinds of game, and surrounded by a crowd of pipers playing national airs. When he has driven out these nuisances, Dicæ-opolis asks the Bœotian what he has brought to market; and the new-comer, in striking contrast with the starved Megarian, enumerates beasts, birds, and dainties of every description. Dicæopolis agrees to purchase the whole pack, in exchange for that Athenian specialty, a "sycophant" or informer—one of those well-abused officials whose duty it was to inform against the importation of contraband goods. At this moment Nicharchus enters, and proceeds to denounce the Bœotian for bringing into the city a wick, which, as he gravely explains, *might* be used for burning down the dockyard. However, he is promptly seized, bound hand and foot, packed up in straw like so much crockery, and carried off under the Bœotian's arm. The Chorus chant a panegyric upon Dicæopolis, and express their hatred of war in an Ode to Peace, or Reconciliation.

And now the Herald comes forth to announce the Feast of Pitchers, in which a skin of wine is given to the most successful tippler. Dicæopolis is very busy preparing for the banquet, and refuses everybody a share of his peace, except a bride who wants to keep her newly married husband from the war. Lamachus is ordered out to keep the passes in the snow, and Dicæopolis receives an invitation to dinner; and the preparations of the two for feasting and fighting are absurdly contrasted.

When Lamachus has departed to keep guard, and Dicæ-opolis to make merry, the Chorus take occasion to abuse Antimachus, who had offended their master, and express a wish that two humorous disasters will befall him.

And now we have reached the closing scene. The warrior and the peacemaker return—the former wounded and miserable, the latter amorous, drunk, and happy; for has he not been triumphant over all rivals and won the drinker's prize? So the play ends, Lamachus limping off to the doctor's, while Dicæopolis is borne away on the shoulders of his companions in joyful procession.

DRAMATIS PERSONÆ.

DICÆOPOLIS, *the good Citizen, an Athenian Farmer.*
Herald.
Prytanies.
Athenian Ambassadors to the Persian Court.
AMPHITHEÜS.
PSEUDARTABAS, *the King of Persia's " Eye."*
THEORUS, *an Athenian Ambassador.*
Chorus of old Acharnians.
Wife of DICÆOPOLIS.
Daughter of DICÆOPOLIS.
EURIPIDES, *the Tragic Poet.*
EURIPIDES' *Slave.*
LAMACHUS, *the Athenian General.*
A Megarian.
Two Daughters of the Megarian.
NICHARCHUS, *an Informer.*
A Bœotian and Boy.
A Bridesman and Bridesmaid.
A Countryman.
   Messengers, Servants, etc.

THE ACHARNIANS

OF

ARISTOPHANES.

Scene—*The Pnyx at Athens.*

Dicæopolis, *alone.*

Dic. There really is no end to my vexations!
My pleasures are too scanty for my patience!
I've only had some four that I could swear to,
While plagued with all the ills that flesh is heir to.
When had I, now, a pure poetic pleasure?
Ah, yes, I know what charmed me beyónd measure;—
To see base Cleon, by that lawsuit shaken,
Disgorging the five talents he had taken.
That made me radiant! The Knights be blest!
They fined the sinner, and the land had rest.*
But then I've had a tragical disaster!
When I sat yawning, waiting for the Master, †
And the man bellowed out, "Lead on the chorus,

---

* This is a parody on a verse of Euripides—

"So may he perish, and the land have rest."

† Dicæopolis was sitting in the theatre, expecting to hear a drama of Æschylus, when a play of Theognis was announced instead. The chilling effect of this poet's productions was so intense, that Aristophanes attributes

Theognis!" Fancy what a shock passed o'er us!
Yet how Dexitheüs pleased me, who just now
Sang the Bœotian, and bore off the cow!*
But I'd this year a paralytic seizure—
When slouching Chæris played the stately measure!
Then never since my mother washed me first,
Was the dust, smarting in my eyes, so curst
As now, when the Assembly's due this minute,
And there's the Pnyx without a creature in it!
They're chattering in the Market-Place, and flying
In all directions from the scarlet dyeing.†
The very Prytanies aren't here;—they'll rush in
At the eleventh hour. Pushing and crushing
To get at the best seats, like streams they roll on!
For peace they never care. O town of Solon!
I'm always *very* first on these occasions,
And take my seat alone, and try my patience;
And groan and gape, and don't know what to do,
Pluck out stray hairs, and do a sum or two.
Then, gazing on the fields, for peace I yearn;
Hating the town, and longing to return

to them the unusual severity of the winter in Thrace (p. 8), and he was nicknamed "Snow." Those who have braved the discomfort of an English concert to hear some famous singer, and have been informed by the polite conductor that the great man is suffering from a cold and therefore unable to sing that evening, will doubtless sympathize with the disappointment of the honest Athenian.

* As a bull was the prize in dithyrambic contests, so a heifer may have been originally the prize for musical competition. But it is probably a mere jest that awards the "harmless necessary cow" for a dull and prosaic *Bœotian* melody.

† If the people were remiss in coming to the assemblies, two archers, or constables, were appointed, who took a rope dyed with vermilion and marked therewith the backs of all whom they found loitering; and those who were found with their backs so marked had to pay a certain fine.

To my own deme,* which never thought of crying,
"Buy coals!" "Buy vinegar!" nor dreamt of buying—
That's *bye*-play to your independent peasant.
And so, to tell the truth, I'm here at present
To shout and jeer and interrupt the speaking,
Unless it's peace and nothing else they're seeking,

Enter Prytanies, Herald, AMPHITHEÜS, *and* Citizens.

Here come the **Prytanies**, at midday too,
Scrambling for places as I said they'd do!
   Herald. Come forth!
Come forth within the ground that's consecrate!
   Amph. Has any speech been made?
   Herald.   Who wants to orate?
   Amph. I do.
   Herald.   Who're you?
   Amph.   Amphitheüs.
   Herald.   Not a human?
   Amph. No, an Immortal, though my ma's a woman.
Thus: (*pompously, burlesquing the genealogical prologues of
      Euripides*) "I whom mortals call Amphitheüs
Sprang from Demeter and Triptolemus.
For they had issue Celeüs, and he
Espoused my grandmother Phænarete;
Her son, Lycinus, was my honoured father,"—
Whence my immortal lineage you'll gather.
The gods have given me a special charter
To go alone and make a peace with Sparta;
But, though my godlike nature no pretence is,

---

   * Attica was divided into more than a hundred "demes" or parishes. Dicæopolis belonged to the deme of Achænæ, eight miles from Athens.
   † The name implies "god on both sides;" hence the herald's question.

I cannot pay my travelling expenses:
The Prytanies don't give——
 Herald.   What ho! the bowmen!
 [*The* Bowmen, *or constables, enter and remove the* "*ob-structionist.*"
 Amph. (*as he is being dragged out*). Triptolemus! Defend
  me from my foemen!
 Dic. O Prytanies, you do abuse the Ecclesia,
Ousting the man who wants to make us easier,
To get us peace, and hang up every buckler!
 Herald. Be silent there!
 Dic.   I'll not be such a truckler,
Not till I hear a motion about peace!
 Herald. The Persian Embassy returned to Greece!
 Dic. Persian indeed! Ambassadors are odious!
I hate the peacocks and the way they toady us!

  Enter the Ambassadors *from Persia, fantastically arrayed
    in Oriental costume.*

 Herald. Silence there!
 Dic.   Whew! Ecbatana! What guys!
 Chief Amb. You sent us, you'll remember, to advise
With the Great King upon affairs of weight.—
Euthymenes then filled our chair of state.— *
Two drachmas each per diem were our wages.
 Dic. Oh, those poor drachmas!
 Amb.   Well, we toiled for ages
O'er the Caÿster's plain, camping or creeping
In chairs, with nothing to be done but sleeping!

 * As Euthymenes had been Archon a dozen years before the representation of this play, the wages here mentioned (about 1s. 4d. each per diem) would amount to no inconsiderable sum (nearly £300 each).

'Twas pitiful!

Dic.   And I deserved no pity
When I lay out on straw to guard the city!

Amb. And then they feasted us, and would insist all
That we should drink from cups of gold and crystal
Their strong sweet wine.

Dic.   Men of the city rocky!
Don't you perceive how all these envoys mock ye?*

Amb. For men are not men, to barbarian thinking,
Unless they're great at eating and at drinking.

Dic. No, nor to ours, unless they've 'scaped the gallows!

Amb. In the fourth year we came to the King's palace;
But he was absent on an expedition,
With all his army and his court physician.
Eight months upon the Golden Mountains seated,
He kept an easement.

Dic.   When had he completed
His labours?

Amb.   He arose, and marching down,
At full of moon returned into the town,
And feasted us, and set before us oxen
All roasted whole in ovens.

Dic.   Now, a pox on
The braggart! Fancy cooking such a—fable!

Amb. Ay, and, by Jove, a bird came on the table
Three times as big as—as Cleonymus yonder—

   [*Points to a very stout gentleman among the audience.*

---

* The complaints of the Ambassador resemble those of Scapin: "Il nous a fait mille civilités, nous a donné la collation, où nous avons mangé des fruits les plus excellents qui se puissent voir, et bu du vin que nous avons trouvé le meilleur du monde." "Qu'y a-t-il de si affligeant à tout cela?" we ask with Géronte of both grumblers.—Molière, "Les Fourberies de Scapin," Acte ii. Scene 11.

A kind of gull it was.
  Dic.   Ah! then no wonder
You gulled us drawing that high salary!
  Amb. And now we've brought with us the Great King's
    Eye,*
Pseudartabas.
  Dic.   I wish a crow'd fly down,
My fine ambassador, and peck your own!
  Herald. The Great King's Eye!

Enter PSEUDARTABAS, *a mask representing one prodigious eye, attended by* Eunuchs.

  Dic.   Great Heracles! Astounding!
You're looking broadsides, man! Pray, are you rounding
A headland into dock till calmer weather?
Why, round your eye you've got a rowlock-leather!
  Amb. Come now, Pseudartabas, to all discover
Why the great King of Persia sent you over.
  Pseud. Beginney shippi-bungo pitchin' hollow!
  Amb. D'ye understand him?
  Dic.   No; I don't quite follow.
  Amb. He says the King will send us gold at once.
  (*To* PSEUD.) Come now, say "gold" again more plain, you
    dunce!
  Pseud. No gettey gole, you blackleggy Ionies!
  Dic. Oh dear! oh dear! how very plain his tone is!
  Amb. He says——

---

* This was the name of the King of Persia's most confidential officers. So the British superintendent in China is called the "barbarian eye."

† This great pantomimic eye resembled the oar-hole of an Athenian man-of-war; hence these allusions.

Dic. We're open to his coarse assertions,
If we expect to get gold from the Persians.
   Amb. No, we'll get gold in *nuggets;* that's the sense.
   Dic. Pshaw! nuggets! You've a pretty impudence!
Stand off, and I will test him if I can.
(*To* Pseud.) You, sir, please tell me,—tell this gentleman,—
                              [*He holds out his fist.*
Briefly and clearly what I wish you to;
And if you don't I'll dye you black and blue.
Now: will the Great King send us any gold?
     [Pseudartabas *and the* Eunuchs *make the Greek sign*
         of negation.
The envoys then have cozened us? We're sold?
     [Pseudartabas *and the* Eunuchs *make the Greek sign*
         of assent.
They nodded Greek! 'Tis plain they come from Hellas!
Ah! but I know now one of those two fellows:—
It's Cleisthines, Sibyrtius's baby!*
Why do you come to us like this, you gaby?
Why don't you shave your beard, you grinning monkey,
Before you personate a Persian flunkey?
   Herald. Silence! Be seated!
The senators invite the Eye to dinner
In the Town Hall!
   Dic. As I'm a living sinner,
This is the very gallows! Here I'm puzzling!
While the door's never shut against *their* guzzling!
But I will do a deed of might and glory!
Where's my Amphitheüs?

   * Cleisthines was a feeble and effeminate creature, who is here called the son of Sibyrtius, a wrestling-master, on the *lucus a non lucendo* principle.

Amph. (*entering on the instant*). He stands before ye!
Dic. Here, take me these eight drachmas * then, and sign
A truce with Sparta for myself and mine,
For my good woman and the little bodies.
                                    [*Exit* AMPHITHEÜS.
(*To the* Prytanies) Keep up your embassies, you gaping noddies!
  Herald. Enter Theorus from Sitalces.

                  Enter THEORUS.

Theor.   Hollo!
  Dic. Another traveller's tale for us to swallow!
  Theor. We should not have remained in Thrace such ages—
  Dic. Not if you hadn't had such handsome wages!
  Theor. But the streams froze, and all the land lay under
A canopy of snow.
  Dic.   Why, yes, no wonder;
Theognis' play was freezing hard just then!
  Theor. Well, all this time I stayed there, gentlemen,
Drinking with Prince Sitalces. There's a frantic
Atheno-maniac for you! So romantic
In his devotion to you, that he'd cover
The walls with scribbling like a crazy lover.—

      "From the east to western sea
        Athens is the fairest She"—

And then his son, whom we had dubbed Athenian,
Desired to taste, being very weak and leany, an
Ionian sausage from the Revels,† sueing

    * About five shillings.
    † The great festival of the Apaturia, peculiar to the Ionic race.

His father to assist the land they grew in.
His father swore, with many a libation,
He'd send the biggest army in the nation,
And make Athenians cry, with hands uplifted,
"Why, what a lot of locusts hither drifted!"

Dic. May I be hanged, if we're not hocus-pocused
By all you say—except that one word "locust." *

Theor. And now he sends you—which I'm sure must charm
    ye—
The fierce and valiant Odomantian army!

Dic. Oh yes! They're come to eat our victuals for us!

Herald. Enter the Thracians brought us by Theorus!

Enter the Thracians, *a troop of wretched tatterdemalions.*

Dic. Pray, what atrocities are these?

Theor.   The host
Of Odomantians. At a trifling cost—
Two drachmas each—they'll desolate with ravages
Bœotia.

Dic. What! Two drachmas for those savages!
You'd have some grumbling from our gallant seamen,†
The city's bulwark! ‡ O my evil demon!
It's *me* they're ravaging! My garlic's gone!
(*To the* Thracians) Put down my garlic!

Theor.   Stop, you simpleton!
They're garlic-valiant now—don't go too near! §

---

   * Dicæopolis means that he has no doubt they will be as ravenous and destructive, if not as numerous, as locusts.

   † The pay of the common sailor was only four obols a day; the Odomantians want two drachmæ, or twelve obols.

   ‡ Athens, like England, owed not only her safety, but also her great empire, mainly to the excellence of her navy.

   § The Greeks used to train their fighting-cocks on garlic.

Dic. You, Prytanies! D'ye see me pillaged here,
In my own country and by foreign losels?
But I forbid a meeting for proposals
About the Thracians' pay: 'tis most profane
The gods declare. I felt a drop of rain!

Herald. Thracians, depart, and two days hence return!
Now, citizens, the meeting will adjourn!

[*Exeunt* Prytanies, Thracians, Theorus, Herald, *and* Citizens.

Dic. Oh, what a salad's wasted on that Tartar!—
But here's Amphitheüs come back from Sparta.
Welcome, Amphitheüs!

Enter Amphitheüs, *running.*

Amph. Not till I stop running!
For I must baffle these Acharnians' cunning.

Dic. Why, what's the matter?

Amph. I was hurrying here
With truces, when some old Acharnians near
Got scent of them, tough hearts of oak and maple—
Old heroes of the Marathonian staple—
And they all bawled and bellowed, "Stop, you lown!
Do you bring truces with our vines cut down?"
Then, while they filled with stones the cloaks they wore,
I ran away, and they pursued and swore.

Dic. Well, let them swear! But you have brought the truces?

Amph. Ay, that I have—three different sample-juices![*]

[*Produces three wine-jars from under his cloak.*

---

[*] A truce was concluded among the Greeks by pouring out libations of wine, and the same word was applied to the libation and to the peace which

Here's one for five years; come, take that and try it.
  Dic. Bah! [*After putting the jar to his lips makes a wry face.*
  Amph. Well?
  Dic. What nasty stuff! I'll never buy it!
It smells of pitch and rigging out new galleys!
  Amph. Then try this ten-year peace.
  Dic. (*tasting it*). It smells of malice
And shilly-shallying among the allies,
And has a powerful stink of embassies!
  Amph. But here's a truce for you by sea and land
For thirty years!
  Dic. (*taking a long pull*). By Jupiter! that's grand!
The genuine smack of nectar and ambrosia!
Most excellent good! It couldn't make things cosier!
It isn't to get ready three days' rations,
But cries out loud, "Pursue your inclinations!"
I'll pour libations out, and drain it dry,
And wish these old Acharnians good-bye.
I go to keep the country feast of Bacchus *
Freed from the wars and miseries that wrack us!
  [*Exit* DICÆOPOLIS.
  Amph. And I'll go too, lest these Acharnians track us!
  [*Exit* AMPHITHEÜS.

Enter the Chorus of old Acharnians, *running.*

Chorus.

Follow this way all together! Ask of every one you meet
If he's seen the rascal running with his truces down the street!

---

it symbolized. Consequently Amphitheüs is enabled to bring the truces with him bodily, in the form of wine-jars, three samples of which he offers for Dicæopolis to taste.

* The feast of the vintage, celebrated in December, a month before the production of this play.

For our city's name and honour we must hunt the fellow down.
Tell me, where's the scoundrel hiding who brings truces to
    the town?
    He's escaped! He's escaped! He has bolted and fled!
    Oh, my feeble old joints, for the years that are sped,
    When I ran with a coal-scuttle tied on my back,
    And was pressing Phayllus himself all the track!*
    Ah! had I but hunted this peace-bearer then,
    He'd never have fled with such ease to his den.
Now my limbs are growing weaker; old Lacratides is sore
With a stiffness in the haunches that he never felt of yore,
So he's gone: but we must chase him! Never let him laugh
    and jeer
At escaping from Acharnians, though their limbs are old and
    queer!
    Father Zeus! Gods above! He has treated with those
    Whom I hate and detest as my bitterest foes!
    Growing fiercer and fiercer, our war never drops
    Until I'm revenged for the loss of my crops;
    Till painful and sharp to the heart of their lines
    Like a bulrush I pierce in defence of my vines!
But we must pursue and chase him; seek him all the wide world
    o'er!
Looking to the plain of *Peltæ*, tracking him from shore to
    shore!
Till at length we find the rascal; for I shall not rest content,
Till at once my *pelting* gives him death and grave and monu-
    ment!

* Phayllus was a mighty runner, who was reported to have jumped fifty-five feet, and to have thrown the *discus* ninety-five. If so, he must first have thrown the quoit over a cliff, and then have jumped after it.

Enter DICÆOPOLIS, *with his* Wife, Daughter, *and* Maid-servant.

Dic. Speak no word of evil omen!

Chorus.

Hush! You hear his prayer for silence! He's the very man,
    I say.
Come to sacrifice, I take it. Let us keep out of the way!
                                        [*The* Chorus *retire.*

Dic. Speak no word of evil omen!
Now, basket-girl,* step forward once or twice!
   Wife. Put down the basket, child; let's sacrifice.
   Daughter. Please, mother, may I have the spoon, to take
The porridge out and pour it on this cake?
   Dic. Now all is well. O Bacchanalian king!
Accept with joy the offerings I bring!
Accept my little family procession,
And keep me free from service and oppression,
That I may keep thy feast and live in clover
Until my thirty years of peace are over!
   Wife. Come, bear the basket prettily, my pretty!
With a proper Sunday face! Don't let 'em loot ye
Of all your gold and jewels in the scrimmage!
   Dic. Now, Xanthias, lift up the Phallic image;
I'll follow with the hymn. You, wife, must now stop,
To make an audience for us, on the housetop.
      [*Exit* Wife. DICÆOPOLIS, *his* Daughter, *and* Maid-
         servant *march in solemn procession round the stage,
         while* DICÆOPOLIS *sings the Phallic hymn.*

---

* Young girls used to walk in the festal processions at Athens, bearing baskets of fruit and sacrificial cakes upon their heads.

THE HYMN.

Hail, Phales! frolic mate of Bacchus!
Whose wandering crews so oft attack us
With many a drunken midnight fracas
  And theft clandestine!
Thou half undo'st the ills that wrack us
  With mirth and jesting!

For five long years I've had hard measure,*
And now come home with heartfelt pleasure
To taste this truce—the dearest treasure
  To us poor haymakers.
No general war shall mar my leisure;—
  Nor General Lamachus! †

'Tis sweeter far than warlike glory
To find your lassie dear before ye,
Roaming 'mid Phelleus' olives hoary,
  In still recesses,
And tell her all your tender story,
  With sweet caresses.

O Phales, drunken, rattling fellow!
When evening cups have made you mellow,
Rose-drops of peace shall chase the yellow
  From morning peepers!
Your shield we'll hang where sparkles tell o'
  Home-fireside keepers!
  [*The* Chorus *rush forward upon* DICÆOPOLIS.

---

* This was the sixth year of the Peloponnesian war.

† This gallant soldier, whose loss was severely felt in the Sicilian expedition, comes in for a great deal of ridicule subsequently, as representative of the war party.

Chor. That's the fellow! That's the man!
   Pelt him! Pelt him! Pelt him there!
   Beat the blackguard now you can!
   Would you spare? Would you spare?

Dic. (*who, leaving his head unguarded, devotes all his care to the preservation of his sacrificial jar*). Heracles! What is the matter? Oh! You'll break my little jar!

Chor. Oh, we'll break your headpiece for you, dirty scoundrel that you are!

Dic. Nay, but tell me what my crime is, reverend Acharnian band.

Chor. You ask *that*, you wretch, you villain! traitor to your fatherland!
You who made a private truce and now can look us in the face!

Dic. But you don't know why I made it. Listen, and I'll state my case.

Chor. Listen to your lies and quibbles? Wretch! We'll bury you with stones!

Dic. Nay, but not until you've heard me. Wait till then to break my bones!

Chor.   I'll not wait: don't you prate
   Any longer; for I hate you!
   Greater scamp than Cleon rate you,—
   Whom to shoe-soles I shall pare,
   For the gallant Knights to wear! *
I won't hear you! I won't listen while you make a long oration;
You have made a peace with Sparta, and must give us compensation!

Dic. Now, my masters, put the question of the Spartans out of sight;

---

* This threat was amply fulfilled next year in the author's "Knights," in which play Cleon, the tanner and demagogue, is most severely satirized.

And just listen to my treaties : judge if I was wrong or right.
 Chor. How can you persist in saying you were right, when you allege
You made peace with men who honour neither altar, oath, nor pledge?
 Dic. Well, I'm sure those Spartans even we so furiously hate
Aren't to blame for all the evils that have fallen on the State.
 Chor. Not for all, you wretch ! you rascal ! Do you dare to tell us so
Freely, flatly to our faces, and then think we'll let you go?
 Dic. Not to blame for all our troubles ; nay, I'd show you, if I might,
They have been in many cases actually in the right !
 Chor. You provoke my soul to frenzy ! You're a traitor to the State,
If you dare to plead before us for the enemies we hate !
 Dic. But if I should plead unfairly ;—if the people scout my plea ;—
While I speak I'll lay my head down on a chopping-block, d'ye see ?
 Chor. Oh, why spare your stones, my demesmen ? Why not pound the loathsome pest?
Why not card and comb the fellow to a right rich purple vest?
 Dic. How the black coal in your spirit leapt to fiery life again !
But, my dear Acharnians, won't you, won't you really hear me then ?
 Chor. No, we won't—we'll never hear you !
 Dic.   Awful, then, will be my lot !
 Chor. I'll be hanged if I will hear you !
 Dic.   Dear Acharnians, I hope not !
 Chor. You shall die upon the spot !

Dic. Then, by Jove, I'll make you smart!
I'll revenge myself by slaying what is dearest to your heart;
For I have a hostage from you, who shall live or die with me.
 Chor. Tell me, tell me, fellow demesmen, what this threat
  of his can be!
Can he have a young Acharnian baby held in durance vile?
Or does his presumption spring from any other act of guile?
 Dic. Stone me, if you like, but I will kill this darling of your
  soul;
Quickly learning who amongst you feels the native love for—
 coal! *

  [*As he pronounces the last word,* DICÆOPOLIS *produces a
  coal-scuttle dressed in long clothes to represent a baby,
  and prepares to pierce it with his sword.*

Chor. (*in great agitation*). We are done for! Do not kill him!
  Our own demesman! Oh, forbear!
Oh, that scuttle! Do not harm him! Spare him, we beseech
 thee, spare!
 Dic. Bawl away, for I shall slay him. I'll not hear you, on
  my soul.
 Chor. Oh, mine own familiar comrade! Oh, my noble heart
  of coal!
 Dic. But just now you would not hear me speak a word
  about the peace.
 Chor. Speak it now, and praise the Spartans to the top of
  your caprice!
For I never will prove traitor to my little scuttle here!

---

 * The Acharnians, who lived hard by the wooded slopes of Mount Parnes, were famous charcoal-burners, and this threat of Dicæopolis appealed to all their most sacred professional instincts. The whole scene is a burlesque upon the "Telephus," a lost play of Euripides, in which one of the characters produced a royal infant, whom he threatened to pierce with his sword unless he was granted a hearing.

Dic. First of all, then, throw your stones down, and I'll spare
   the little dear.
Chor.   See! we've thrown them all away!
   Now put up your sword, I pray.
Dic.   But take care you try no hoax!
   Hide no pebbles in your cloaks!
Chor.   See, they're shaken on the ground,
   Shaken by our dancing round!
   Now, don't prate another word,
   But make haste and sheathe the sword!

[*The* Chorus *dance round and shake out the stones from
their cloaks, while* DICÆOPOLIS *puts away the sword
and the coal-scuttle.*

Dic. So then, you could at last shake out your—breath!
Parnesian charcoal nearly died the death
Through its own deme's unnatural misdoing!
It was so frightened that it fell to spewing
A lot of coal-dust, like a cuttle-fish!
'Tis monstrous sad men bear such acidish
And sour-grape natures, that they pelt and laugh
To utter scorn your decent half-and-half!
And even when I'm offering to lay
My head upon a block and say my say!
And yet I love my life as well as they!

1st *Semi-Chorus.*

Why, then, don't you bring the block out from within,
   And begin?
I am mightily desirous to know what you have to say!
   Speak away!

2nd Semi-Chor. Yes, since the penalty's of your own seeking,
Bring here the chopping-block, and try your speaking.

[DICÆOPOLIS *fetches a chopping-block.*

Dic. See! Here's the block, and here's the little, weak,
Unhappy mortal who is going to speak!
Jove! I shan't take a buckler, never fear it!
But say just what I think of Spartan merit!
And yet—I'm very much afraid! I'm versed in
The humours of these rustics, always thirsting
To hear some quack with fulsome adulation
Bespattering themselves and all the nation.
What matter whether lies or truth be told—
They never know how they are being sold!
And then I know your old man—how he gloats
O'er nothing like condemnatory votes!
And I remembered how *I* fared one day
At Cleon's hands, for last year's comic play.*
How to the Senate House he pulled and dragged me,
And battered me with calumnies, and nagged me,
And spattered me with muddy jokes and sallies,
While on my head he rinsed his dirty malice,
And swore such water-spouts, I nearly died
Draggled and drowned in that polluting tide!
So now, before I speak, let me assume
Some tragical and beggarly costume.
  Chor. Why these twists and shifts, I pray?
     Why this craving for delay?
Get Hieronymus to lend you one of Hades' casques to wear,
   With its "murkily-shaggily-clustering hair," †

---

 * Dicæopolis is, of course, speaking in the person of Aristophanes, who had been prosecuted by Cleon for some strong expressions of feeling contained in his comedy of "The Babylonians." Cleon also called in question the poet's right of citizenship; but Aristophanes escaped by a witticism, quoting the Homeric line, "It's a wise child that knows its own father."

 † The helmet of Hades was supposed to confer invisibility upon the wearer, and it is thus appropriately attributed to Hieronymus, a tragic poet

> I don't care:
> Or Sisyphus' tricks you may try if you choose; *—
> But this trial will not admit any excuse.

Dic. 'Tis time for me to take good heart of grace!
For I must look Euripides i' the face!†

   [*He knocks at the door of a house at the back of the stage.*
Porter!

Porter (opening the door). Who's there?

Dic.   Euripides indoors?

Porter (after a moment's reflection). Indoors, and out of doors, if sense is yours!

Dic. Why, how can he be in yet out, you dunce? ‡

---

who concealed himself in a cloud of words, a specimen of which is here given.

* The most celebrated feat of Sisyphus is thus mentioned by Theognis:

> "No; not if than Sisyphus' self you were wiser
> Who even from Tartarus drear
> Found a means of escaping, the crafty deviser,
> By tickling Persephone's ear!"

† Throughout the following scene there are many allusions which can only be explained by a reference to the dramas of Euripides. All the "beggars and cripples" mentioned, with their various accoutrements, may be found therein; and Aristophanes was too strong a conservative and too incorrigible a satirist not to regard such "touches of things common" from the comic point of view. All the quotations are samples of the Euripidean "word-craft," that new-fangled subtlety of expression which marked the analytic and casuistical spirit of the times.

‡ " *Tal.* No, no, I am but shadow of myself:
You are deceived, my substance is not here;
For what you see is but the smallest part
And least proportion of humanity:
I tell you, madam, were the whole frame here,
It is of such a spacious lofty pitch,
Your roof were not sufficient to contain it!
   Count. This is a riddling merchant for the nonce!
He will be here, and yet he is not here!
How can these contrarieties agree?
   Tal. That will I show you presently."
SHAKESPEARE (?), *King Henry VI.*, *Part I.*, Act ii. sc. 3.

Porter (*with the alacrity of a sophist scenting a metaphysical argument*). I'll prove you, master, that he's both at once.
Abroad his intellectual being soars
Collecting verselets, and is out of doors:
His "vital presence" and material man
Sits in the garret, making verses scan.
 Dic. Euripides is lucky, I declare,
To have a porter who can split a hair !*
Call him.
 Porter. But that can't be.
 Dic. But else you'll rue it,
For I shall stay here knocking till you do it!
Euripides ! my Euripidion!
Hear me, if ever you heard any one !
It's Dicæopolis from Chollidæ !
 Eur. (*within*). But I'm engaged !
 Dic. But let them wheel you free !
 Eur. But that can't be !
 Dic. But if you don't you'll rue it !
 Eur. But, being too busy to come down, I'll do it !
          [EURIPIDES *is wheeled out in the encyclema.*†
 Dic. I say, Euripides !
 Eur. Well, what d'ye say ?
 Dic. Why, so you make your plays up there all day,
Instead of the ground floor ! Well, that should teach us
Why all of them go lame before they reach us,

---

* Contrast.—"As I was sitting in my chamber, and thinking on a subject for my next *Spectator*, I heard two or three irregular bounces at my landlady's door, and upon the opening of it, a loud cheerful voice inquiring whether the philosopher was at home. The child who went to the door answered very innocently, that he did not lodge there."—*Spectator.*

† The *encyclema* was a semi-circular machine which was wheeled out from an opening at the back of the stage, some little distance above the ground.

Verses and characters alike !   And, pray,
Why wear those tatters from some tragic play,
Those "weeds of woe"?   Well, that should teach us why
They're both alike so very beggarly !
But, dear Euripides, I beg and pray,
Give me a little rag from that old play :
For I must make a long speech to the chorus,
And "if we fail"—our life must answer for us !

Eur. What tatters would you?   Those my Œneus there,
"The old man dismal-fated," used to wear ?

Dic. Not Œneus, no ; a wretcheder than Œneus !

Eur. Blind Phœnix ?

Dic.   No, although *his* rags had seen use.
But there was one e'en wretcheder than he !

Eur. What "shreds of raiment" would the fellow see ?
D'ye mean the rags of beggar Philoctetes?

Dic. No ; my man's beggary far more complete is !

Eur. Would you the "muddy vesture" that went on
The crippled limbs of that Bellerophon ?

Dic. No, not Bellerophon ; but just that stamp,—
A lame, persistent, prating, prosing tramp.

Eur. I know him !   Telephus !

Dic.   Ay, Telephus ! *
Give me his swaddlings and be generous !

Eur. (*to his slave*).   Boy, bring him Telephus's tattered
         tags !
You'll find them lying on Thyestes' rags,
Just under Ino's.

Slave.   Take them !   They are here !

---

* "Telephus, Prince of Mysia," was the title of a play of Euripides, which has not come down to us, and we cannot therefore estimate the accuracy of the portrait which the poet himself is here so quick to recognize.

Dic. (*holding the garments up to the light to show their "loop'd
    and windowed raggedness"*). By Jove! They'll *see
    through* this disguise, I fear!
But 'tis indeed most tragically designed!
Euripides, as you have been so kind,
Pray give me all belonging to the suit,
The Mysian bonnet for my head, to boot.
"Since I this day must play the beggar here,
Be what I am but some one else appear!"
While all the audience know that I am *I*.
But each poor foolish chorus-man stands by
For me to flip my "word-craft" at his nose!

Eur. I will; "the webs of thought thou weavest close!"

Dic. "Bless *you;* may Telephus be—*what I trow!*"
Bravo! What "word-craft" I'm being filled with now!
But still I want a little beggar's stick.

Eur. Take it; and leave the "marble mansion" quick!

Dic. O soul! thou'rt ousted from these halls of his,
Though still in want of many properties!
So now thou must be firm, and persevere,
And importune.—Euripides, my dear,
Give me a tiny basket with a handle—
One with a hole burnt through it by a candle!

Eur. What want then of this woven thing is thine?

Dic. Why, none at all; I *want* it—to be mine.

Eur. "Evacuate the palace," and don't bother!

Dic. May Heaven bless you—as it blessed your mother!*

Eur. Now, sir, begone!

Dic.   But grant me one more whim,

---

* This is a very left-handed benediction, since the poet's mother passed her life behind a greengrocery stall. Hence the request for a "lettuce," as an appropriate family heirloom.

A little pitcher with a broken rim.
    Eur. There, take it with my curse, "plague of the palace."
    Dic. By Jove! to his own plaguiness he's callous!
But give me one thing more, a little jug—
There's a good darling—with a sponge for plug!
    Eur. Fellow, you'll rob me of my tragedy!
Take it and go!
    Dic.   I'm going;—yet, dear me!
What shall I do? I want just *one* thing more,
And then I'll go for ever. I implore,
Euripides—for very life I ask it—
Give me some withered leaves to line the basket!
    Eur. There! there! You'll ruin me! My plays are
        "sped"!
    Dic. No more; I'm going: for my "hardihead"
Is over great, "nor recks of royal loathing."—
Oh dear! Poor me! I'm lost and brought to nothing!
I'm done for! I forgot the corner-stone
Of all my fortunes!—Euripidion,
Sweetest and best of men, I thee implore!
May I be hanged if I ask any more,
But this one, single trifle, and no other—
Just one poor lettuce, "heirloom of thy mother!"
    Eur. The man insults us. "Close the barriers," there!
                                 [EURIPIDES *is wheeled in.*
    Dic. Poor soul, without a lettuce thou must fare!
Now do the dangers of the race dishearten
A soul that's going to speak up for the Spartan?
Here is the scratch! Come forth, my soul, and toe it!
Dost halt? Hast thou not drunk—the piteous poet?
That's right: and now go yonder, "poor my heart,"
And lay your head down there to speak your part,

Screw up your courage! Eyes upon the goal!
Art ready? Go! Well done, my noble soul!

1st Semi-Chorus.

What shall you say? What is your plan?
Shameless, insolent, brazen man!
To pledge the State your neck, as you have done,
Defending a minority of one!

2nd Semi-Chorus.

He does not fear his task to-day!
Since you have chosen it, speak away!
Dic. "Take it not ill," spectators, "I beseech,"
That "though a beggar" I shall make a speech
Before Athenians upon State concerns
In comic style: e'en Comedy discerns
The claims of justice, and what I shall say
Will be severe, but just; and yet to-day
Cleon will not accuse me with his jeer
That I abuse the State with strangers here.*
At this Lenæan feast we're quite alone;
The strangers haven't come yet; there are none
Arrived with tribute, and no troops as yet
From the allies; so now at least we're met
All by ourselves, clean-husked Athenians born,—
For as to Metics, they're the chaff o' the corn!†
Now, *I* hate Spartans very much indeed,
And wish the ocean-god, whose victims bleed

---

* It appears that Cleon, in his accusation of Aristophanes before referred to, had made a point by insisting on the fact that "The Babylonians" was performed at the great Dionysian festival in March, when the city was crowded with strangers, and when the libel would be consequently more gross.

† The "Metics" were resident but non-naturalized foreigners.

On Tænarum, would make their houses fall,
Shaken by earthquakes, down upon them all !
For *I've* had vines cut down as well as others.
But—since all present here are friends and brothers—
Why blame the Spartans for this inconvenience?
For there are men with us—but not Athenians,—
I never said they were *Athenians*, mind !—
Not *men* at all, but wretched, ill-designed
False counterfeits, the current coin debased,*
Flash citizens, dishonoured and disgraced,
Who confiscated the Megarians' jerkins !
And if they sighted garlic, salt or girkins,
Lev'rets or sucking-pigs, they called them "ware
From Megara," and sold them then and there !
That was a custom native to the land ;
'Twas graver matter when a drunken band
Of cottabus-befuddled † boys went over
And stole a girl from her Megarian lover.
Then the Megarians, bursting with vexation,
Steal from Aspasia in retaliation
Two other doxies ; and the war that drenches
All Greece with blood was due to these three wenches ! ‡

* "An't please your Majesty, we have brought you here a slip, a piece of false coin : one that is neither stamped with true coin for his excuse nor with good clothes for his redemption."—"The Dumb Knight," Act v. sc. 1.

† The "cottabus" was a game, which consisted in throwing the wine left at the bottom of the cups into a metal dish, often placed at some distance from the thrower, without spilling any on the ground. As this pastime required a great number of heel-taps, and necessitated the consumption of a good deal of liquor, it was very popular with young Athens.

‡ Those who believe that "if the nose of Cleopatra had been an inch shorter the destinies of the whole world would have been changed," will perhaps find as much truth in this gossiping account of "Pericles the Olympian" being roused by the wrongs of his mistress Aspasia, as in the sober pages of the historian who ignores her existence.

For then the Olympian Pericles in ire
Fulmined and lightened with vindictive fire,*
And shook all Hellas with his armèd throngs,
And laid down laws that read like drinking-songs,— †
"That the Megarians do no more remain
On land, or market-place, or sea, or plain!"
Then the Megarians, when famine's stride
Came nearer, begged the Spartans to provide
That the Three-Women Bill should be repealed;
But, though they often begged, we would not yield;
And thence arose the clatter of the shield.

    You'll say, "'Twas wrong." But what was right, I pray?
Come now, suppose a Spartan, some fine day,
Sailed to Seriphus, and gave information,
And sold—a puppy-dog to your vexation!
Would you have stayed at home? No, that you'd not!
The truth is, you'd have launched upon the spot
Three hundred galleys, filled the town with bawling
For ship-owners and captains, soldiers calling,
With pay being given, measuring of rations,
Figure-heads gilded, groaning trading-stations,
With thongs and wine-skins, people buying firkins,
Garlic-heads, olives, nets of onions, girkins,
Chaplets, sprats, bruises, piping-women, scars;

    * "Whose resistless eloquence
Wielded at will that fierce democratie,
Shook the arsenal, and fulmined over Greece."
        MILTON, *Paradise Regained*, Bk. iv.

  † There is a special allusion to a drinking-song by Timocrates of Rhodes:—

"O blind Wealth! that thou mightst be
    Never seen again,
On the earth, or on the sea,
    Or the fruitful plain!"

The dockyard had been full of flattening spars,
And banging nails, and fitting oars for griping,
Flutes playing, boatswains whistling, pipers piping.
That you'd have done ; " Deem we that Telephus
Had not? then reason hath departed us !"

   1st Semi-Chor. How dare you, beggar, talk like this, and task all
Informers to our face, you arrant rascal?

   2nd Semi-Chor. Nay, by Poseidon, but the man speaks fair :
All that he says is true, not false, I swear !

   1st Semi-Chor. And if it is, what right has he to speak it?
On his bold head my vengeance shall be wreakèd !

     [*The first* Semi-Chorus *advance in a threatening attitude
towards* DICÆOPOLIS.

   2nd Semi-Chor. (*interposing*). Ho, there ! Where are you running to? Stay ! stay !
If you touch him, *you'll* get a throw, I say.

     [*A struggle takes place between the two divisions of the*
Chorus, *in which the first* Semi-Chorus, *the party
hostile to* DICÆOPOLIS, *is worsted; thereupon it
implores the assistance of* LAMACHUS.

   1st Semi-Chor. (*sings*).

       Lamachus ! Appear ! appear !
        Let the lightning of thine eye
      Strike the foeman's heart with fear !
        Fellow-tribesman, hasten nigh !
      "Bless us now with wishèd sight !"
       Mighty, Gorgon-crested knight !

       Is there here a warrior-form,
         Knight-at-arms or colonel?

Any soldier skilled to storm
    Town and tower impregnable?—
Let him come to aid with haste,—
For I'm grappled round the waist!
[LAMACHUS *strides upon the stage, accoutred like a burlesque hero with rustling plumes and clanging armour.*

Lam. Whence came that martial summons from afar?
Where must I aid? where wake the din of war?
Who roused the Gorgon from her case of leather?
Dic. (*feigning extreme terror*). Sir Lamachus! What fettle and
    what a feather!
1st Semi-Chor. O Lamachus, hasn't this scurvy jack
Been slandering all our State this long time back?
Lam. How? Dares a mendicant like thee talk thus?
Dic. Grammercy! Pardon it, Sir Lamachus!
If a beggar like me did prate and prattle so!
Lam. What saidst thou of us? Speak!
Dic.   I—don't—yet—know!
Your terrible armour makes my head go round!
Oh, please, please put that bugbear on the ground!
Lam. (*laying down his shield*). There, then!
Dic.   Now turn it upside down.
Lam. (*reversing the shield so that the Gorgon-head is undermost*). I've done it.
Dic. Now give me, please, the feather from your bonnet.
Lam. Well, there's the feather.
Dic.   Hold my head awhile;
I don't feel well—those plumes have stirred my bile!*

---

* This scene is a burlesque upon a well-known incident in the Iliad:
    "Thus as he spoke, great Hector stretched his arms
        To take his child; but back the infant shrank,

Lam. Wretch! Wouldst thou use my feather for a vomit?
Dic. What is the bird if that's a feather from it?
It's a white-feathered Boaster, I suppose.*
Lam. Ha! thou shalt die!
Dic.   No, Lamachus; your blows
Don't reach the point between us here at all.
Lam. How, beggar? Speak'st thou thus to a general?
Dic. Am I a beggar?
Lam.   Why, what are you, then?
Dic. What am I? Why, I'm a good citizen,
And not a toadying place-hunter's son:
But, since the war began, the son of a gun,
And not the son of a pay-captain—like you!
Lam. I was elected——
Dic.   By an owl or two! †
Well, I made peace, for I was sick and ill
To see grey-headed veterans serving still,
And boys like you all shuffling off to race—
Some with three drachmas salary to Thrace,

> Crying, and sought his nurse's sheltering breast,
> Scared by the brazen helm and horsehair plume,
> That nodded, fearful, on the warrior's crest.
> Laughed the fond parents both, and from his brow
> Hector the casque removed, and set it down,
> All glittering, on the ground; then kissed his child."
>   Derby's *Iliad*, vi. 543–550.

* "His device was a cock azure with a tail argent, with this motto—

    'I neither strutte nor crowe nor fyghte,
    For why? Because my tail is white.'"

—From an unpublished election squib by the late Lord Macaulay.

† The Greek is "by three cuckoos;" that is, according to one explanation, by three fellows who gave their votes over and over again, so as to seem far more than three, just as when a cuckoo cries the whole place seems full of cuckoos. But probably "cuckoo" was a common term for a stupid fellow, as "owl" is with us.

Your Tisamenophænippæan brothers
And Vagabondhipparchides; and others,
Ceres and Theodorus, to Chaonians
Or Chares, with our Attico-Bezonians,—*
Others to Camarina and to Sicily—
Ay, and to any other place that *is* silly!

Lam. They were elected——

Dic.   Ay, but what's the reason
You're always going, in and out of season,
And getting salaries, and none of these?

                               [*Pointing to the* Acharnians.

Say, did *you* ever go, Marilades,
On an embassy—although you're old enough?
See there! he shakes his head; yet he's your stuff,
A steady working man. And what of these,
Dracyllus, Prinides, Euphorides?
Has any one of you been all the way
To see the Great King, or Chaonia?
They answer, "No!" 'Tis only Lamachus
And Cœsyra's baby † who have prospered thus!
Men who were only yesterday so drowned
In debts and taxes, that their friends would sound
The alarm, "Keep off!" whene'er they came in sight,—
Like people pouring out the slops at night!

---

* These "un-in-one-breath-utterable" words are compounded of the names of persons otherwise quite unknown. "They are the grubs," says Mitchell, "whom the amber of poetry alone preserves in existence." The word translated "Attico-Bezonians" means literally "humbugs from the borough of Diomeiæ," to whom the term "Bezonian," which seems to bear the double meaning of "a new-levied, fresh-water soldier," and "a rascall, a base-humoured scoundrel," seems peculiarly applicable (cf. Shakespeare, "Henry IV., Part II.," Act v. sc. 3).

† The allusion here is quite lost. Some think Alcibiades is meant, who had a maternal ancestress of the name of Cœsyra.

Lam. O sovereign people! Must I bear this, say!
Dic. No—not when Lamachus refuses pay!
Lam. Then will I wage most furious bloody strife
On sea and land throughout my mortal life,
Against all Spartans and their base allies!
With puissant arm I'll strike and scourge mine enemies!
[*Exit* LAMACHUS.

Dic. And I make proclamation unto Sparta
And her allies, that all with me may barter.
Megarians and Bœotians may thus
Come to my market—but not Lamachus! [*Exit* DICÆOPOLIS.

THE PARABASIS.*

I. COMMATION.

He's winning the day, and the people incline
    To the truce; in their conscience his plea sticks.
But we'll doff our long-flowing robes and combine
    To chant out the loud Anapæstics!

II. ANAPÆSTS.

From the time when his first comic chorus was given our
    Master † he never

---

* "The Parabasis" is the most striking and original feature of the old Greek comedy, being the last representative of that primitive comus from which the drama took its rise. The Chorus, consisting of four and twenty persons, turned round from their usual position between the stage and the *thymele*, or altar of Dionysus, which stood in the centre of the orchestra, and passed round to the other side of the altar, singing the Commation. They then stood facing the audience, and, after divesting themselves of their long robes in order to dance with greater ease, proceeded to chant the Anapæsts and following choric odes, which have no connection with the plot of the drama, but are addressed directly from the poet to his hearers.

† The poet whose comedy was to be represented at the festivals was also master of the Chorus, whom he drilled and instructed in their parts.

Has come on the stage to assure us that he is remarkably clever;
But his enemies charged him of late, in Athens of speedy decision,
Of libelling people and State with an insolent scoffing derision,
And so he now wants to reply to Athens of—fickle decision,
Declaring his merits are high and deserving of your recognition.
'Twas he who prevented the State from being fooled by each foreign oration,
From swallowing flattery's bait with an open-mouthed cit's delectation.
Ere that, all the envoys who came from the cities would try to get round you,
Recalling your glorious name and the "violet chaplets" that crowned you—*
When any one uttered the phrase you were all so rejoiced beyond measure
At the "crowns" all united to praise that you sat upon tip-tail for pleasure !
And if any one flattered your pride, to the "sleekness" of Athens referring,
He'd bring all the world to his side by a compliment fit for a herring.
In this way, our master replies, he has done you a service emphatic,
By showing how all the allies are conducting their rule democratic,†

* The epithets "violet-crowned" and "sleek" are bestowed upon the city by Pindar. The first refers to the graceful Athenian custom of wearing wreaths of flowers, especially violets and roses, upon the head; and the second to their habit of anointing themselves with olive oil.

† In "The Babylonians" Aristophanes appears to have taken the Athenians down a peg or two, by contrasting the government existing in the allied states with their own haphazard democracy.

So now they will quickly arrive with the tribute they owe to
    the city,
All eager to see him alive, the poet so brave and so witty;
The poet who risked his own life to Athens her duty declaring.
Yea, now in far countries is rife the fame of his glorious daring;
The King himself lately demanded of some envoys from Sparta
    discreet,*
First, which of the two states commanded the Grecian seas
    with her fleet;
And secondly, which was so often abused by this wonderful
    poet:
"Already their wicked hearts soften to virtue," he said, "and I
    know it;
The side he so wisely advises will soon get the best of the
    blows!"
And this is why Sparta devises proposals of peace for her foes;
For she asks back Ægina—not caring a jot for the island, that's
    clear;
But craftily bent upon tearing our bard from his natural sphere.†
But never do you let him go, for he'll play out his part with
    sincerity,
And promises ever to show the virtuous path to prosperity.
Not fawning nor offering bribes, not tricking nor playing the
    cheat,
Not drenching with long diatribes, but teaching what's honest
    and meet!

    * The monarch in question is the king of the Persian Empire, called always *the* King, par excellence. Of course this is only an amusing "puff." We can hardly infer from it, as one translator of this play does, that "the reputation of our poet was so great that it had reached even to the Persian Court, and induced the powerful monarch of that country to inquire into his native place and abode;" still less that "he was held in great esteem there" (!) (Wheelwright's "Aristophanes," vol. i. p. vii. preface).
    † Aristophanes held some land in the island of Ægina.

III. Macron.

(Pronounced by the actor in a breath.)

And therefore let Cleon exhibit his skill
In plotting against me whatever he will;
"Confederate justice" my bosom shall thrill,
And I'll never, like him, be convicted of ill,
Who was false to the State and is false to it still!

IV. Strophe.

Come, Acharnian Muse, that burnest
  With the fire that feeds thy heart,
Energetic, strong, and earnest
  Is thy native simple art!
Thy live vigour shall not dwindle,
  As the sparks incessant leap
Which the helpful bellows kindle
  From the oak logs' smouldering heap:
When the little fish are lying,
All upon the charcoal frying;
  And, while some are kneading bread,
Others mix the Thasian pickle,
  Pickle, "richly filleted." *
So, I pray thee, be not fickle!
    Bring a song,
Lively, nervous, bold, and strong,
Rough with rustic hardihood,
Come to me, thy demesman good!

---

* Pindar had applied this epithet to the goddess of memory, to whom it was hardly more appropriate than to a Thasian pickle.

V. Epirema.

We the aged, we the hoary, blame the thing our State has done!
That our old age is not cherished, for the sea-fights that we won!
Hard, ungrateful is your conduct! dragging men with age opprest
To be laughed at in the law courts by the stripling's ready jest!
Ancient men, mere living shadows, deaf to sound, with pipe played out,
Whose Poseidon and Preserver is the staff they bear about!
Mumbling, drivelling with dotage, there we stand within our place,
Seeing nothing but the darkness of the labyrinthean case.
Then the youngster, very jealous to conduct his accusation,
Smartly cudgels us with phrases clenched into a neat oration.
Then he drags us up to question, setting all his word-traps baited,
Hounding, pounding, and confounding poor Tithonus evil-fated!—
Toothless with old age he mutters, and at last he goes away,
And the verdict is against him, his accuser wins the day.
Then he sobs and tells his comrades, with a bitter, tearful whine—
"All the money for my coffin must be paid to meet the fine!"

VI. Antistrophe.

Shame upon your evil-doing!
Ye who bring up every day
To the water-clock * and ruin
Some poor fellow, old and grey!

* The water-clock, or hour-glass, which marked the lapse of time in the courts of law, and by which the length of speeches was regulated.

Some old mate who shared your labour,
  Wiping off the manly sweat
From his brow, your constant neighbour
  In the battle's dust and heat;
One with whom you fought and won,
On the field of Marathon.
  We were making charges then
On the foe that backward hurried,
  Now by shameless countrymen
We ourselves are charged and worried;
  Till at last
We're defeated too, and cast.
Who this scandal will deny?
Even Marpsias * dare not try!

VII. ANTEPIREMA.

Should a bent and hoary greybeard like Thucydides † be sued?
Vext by this abomination of a Scythian solitude,
Ruined by this prating pleader, this Cephisodemus here?
Ah! my heart was full with pity and I brushed aside a tear
When I saw a Scythian archer, a long-winded advocate,
Sore perplexing and confounding that old servant of the State:
Who, by Ceres, in the old time when he *was* Thucydides,
From that dame herself would never have endured such wrongs
    as these!

* Who this particular Marpsias was is not known; but he was evidently a lawyer, and so the joke remains.

† This Thucydides was not the great historian, but he may have been that son of Milesias who was the political opponent of Pericles. Cephisodemus is not known to history, and therefore we cannot tell why he is called a "Scythian archer."

Rather would he first have gripped and flung Euathluses* by
    dozens,
Then bawled down ten thousand archers, and outshot his
    father's cousins!
But, since now you will not suffer aged men to sleep in peace,
Vote that suits should be divided, that this great injustice cease.
Let the toothless charge the toothless, let the old accuse the old,
Let the young have smart accusers, ready-tongued and quick
    and bold,
So in future you must never fine or banish those who're flung,
Save when old men sue the old men and when young men sue
    the young!

Enter DICÆOPOLIS.

Dic. These are the bounds, then, of my place of barter
Which I throw open to allies of Sparta.
Megarians and Bœotians may thus
Come to my market—but not Lamachus.
The market stewards I elect together
By lot to be—these three good straps of leather;
And hither let no base informer come,
Nor any other man from Sneakingholm.
Now I'll set up the pillar with the treaty,
And make it visible to all the city.   [*Exit* DICÆOPOLIS.

Enter a Megarian, *with two young* Daughters. †

Meg. Hail! Mart o' Athens, to Megarians dear!
I've yearned for ye, by Friendship's Lord, sae sair

---

    * Nothing is known of Euathlus except that he was a wrangling advocate; the allusions in the next line are quite lost.
    † This Megarian talks in a very broad Doric dialect, the effect of which I have endeavoured to reproduce by the use of Scotch.

As ye'd 'a bin my mither! Hoot! thegither!
Ye misleared bairns of an unlucky feyther!
Gie up, and (gin ye fin' it) pree the haggis!
Just hearkee now wi' a' your empty—baggies;
Wad ye be selt or wad ye starve to death?

Daughters. We wad be selt! selt!

Meg. An' sae I think. But whare'd ye fin', guid faith!
A coof sae feckless as to buy ye baith,
Ye guid-for-naething hizzies! Hech! I've hit on
A guid Megarian plan! I'se gar ye pit on
Thae clouts, and say I've brought twa soos to niffer!
Pit on the pig-graith now, an' dinna differ
Frae braw auld Grumphie's bairns, or, on my aith,
I'se take ye hame at ance to starve to death!
And pit thae snouts here now upon your grunzies;
And gae into this sack at ance, ye dunces;
And mind ye grumph, and say "Koi! Koi!" an' squeal
Like whingin Mystery pigs * an' unco deal.
Now I'se ca' Dicæopolis to choose.—
Hoolie! my mon! an' wad ye buy some soos?

Enter DICÆOPOLIS.

Dic. What's this? A man from Megara?

Meg.   We're come
To market, mon.

Dic.   And how d'ye do at home?

Meg. We sit a' day i' the chimla-lug and—fast!

Dic. Ah! that's delightful, if the liquor last! †
And if a piper's there, that's very pleasant!

---

* Pigs sacrificed to Demeter before initiation into her Mysteries.

† Dicæopolis, unaccustomed to the Doric brogue, understands him to say "feast."

How else do you Megarians fare at present?
    Meg. Jist so-so: when I started to come hither
The council was consultin' a'thegither,
What was the best and quickest gate to—die!
    Dic. Then you will soon be freed from misery!
    Meg. Weel, weel.
    Dic.   What else?   How is corn selling there?
    Meg. It's like the gods wi' us—it's unco *dear!*
    Dic. Then have you salt?
    Meg.   Haen't ye the saut-warks too?
    Dic. Or garlic?
    Meg.   Fient haet garlic hae we noo!
When ye invade our kintra like feal-mice,
Ye howk up a' the heads o' 't, in a trice!
    Dic. What have you, then?
    Meg.   Twa soos for the Mysteries!
    Dic. Good: let me see them.
    Meg.   They're guid soos, are these.
Lift up this ane and feel her, gin ye choose,
How much she weighs.   They're baith maist buirdly soos!
    Dic. (*feeling the sack*). What's this thing?
    Meg.   It's a *soo*, mon.
    Dic.   Of what breed?
    Meg. Megarian.   Isna that a soo indeed?
    Dic. It doesn't look like one to me, it's true.
    Meg. Mair shame t'ye!   Leuk at his suspectin' noo!
He says this is no pig ava!   I'se wad ye,
Some thymit saut noo, an ye wiss, my laddie,
That it's a proper pig by the law o' Greece!
    Dic. Well, it's a proper pig of the human race!
    Meg. Trowth, mon, it's mine—wha's did ye think it was?
Hae ye a min' to hear them squeal?

Dic. Oh yes!
Meg. Be quick now, soo, at ance, and mak' a squeel!
Ye mauna haud your whist, ye ne'er-do-weel,
Or, on my aith, I'se tak ye hame again!
Daughter. Koi! Koi!
Meg. Is that a pig?
Dic. Now it's a pig, that's plain!
But it will be a woman when it's prime.
Meg. It will be like its mither in five years' time.
Dic. But it won't do for sacrifice.
Meg. Why no?
Why won't it do?
Dic. It has no tail to show!
Meg. Weel, it's a young ane—when it's been weel fed,
'Twill hae a guid lang tail a' fat and red.
But an' ye rear it—here's a bonny soo!
Dic. It's very like the other one, it's true!
Meg. They're frae ae mither and ae feyther baith!
'Tis a good Venus offering, i' faith!
Dic. And can they feed without their mother now?
Meg. Ay, and wi'out their feyther, ye may vow!
Dic. What do they eat most?
Meg. A' you'll let 'em try!
Jist speer at them yersel!
Dic. Pigs!
Daughters. Koi! Koi! Koi!
Dic. Would you like peas to eat?
Daught. Koi! Koi! Koi! Koi!
Dic. What, and dried figs from Phibalis?
Daught. Koi! Koi!
Dic. Oh, what a squeal they give when I say "figs"!
Let some one bring out figs for the little pigs.

Now, will they eat them? Heracles! Look there!*
They munch them quite like human beings, I swear!
Whate'er the breed, they're very *gorgeous* pigs!
And yet they cannot have gorged all the figs!

   Meg. Na, na—I jist took this ane for mysel'!

   Dic. They're most humane young porkers, I can tell!
What do you want now for your pigs, my man?

   Meg. I'se ha'e a bunch o' garlic for this ane!
And tak' for tither ane a quart of saut!

   Dic. Stay here: I'll buy them!   [*Exit* DICÆOPOLIS.

   Meg.   Hermes o' the Mart!
Jist let me gae and sell my wifie noo,
This vera gate—and my auld mither too!

         Enter an Informer.

   Inf. Fellow, who're you?

   Meg.   I'm a Megarian, trowth,
A pig-merchant!

   Inf.   Then I'll denounce you both
As enemies, your little pigs and you!

   Meg. The cause of a' our skaith's returnin' noo!

   Inf. I'll teach you, sir, to Megarize like this!
Put down the sack!

   Meg.   Ho! Dicæopolis!
Some ane's denouncin' me!

         Enter DICÆOPOLIS.

   Dic.   Who's that denouncing?
Come, market stewards, you were meant for trouncing
   Informers. (*He belabours the* Informer *with his leather straps.*)
        Who gave you your education,

---

   * Heracles is appealed to as the god of trenchermen.

You dunce ? Pray, how can you give information?
Inf. Shan't I denounce our enemies?
Dic. You'll rue it,
Unless you run off somewhere else to do it !
Meg. Trowth ! What a plague at Athens this maun be !
Dic. Cheer up, Megarian ! Here's the price, you see,
The salt and garlic for the pigs I get !
Take it and fare you well !
Meg. I'll no do thet ;
We fare na weel in my countra !
Dic. Then may it
Recoil on me, if I was wrong to say it !
Meg. My little soos, try now, wi'out your daddie,
To eat your bonnocks sauted—an they're ready !
[*Exeunt omnes.*

Chorus.

The fellow hit a lucky chance ! See how his plan's progressing !
He'll reap a glorious crop of wealth and fame and every
    blessing !
    Yes, in the Market-Place he'll stay.
    And if a Ctesias * steps that way,
        Or any other spy comes prowling—
        He'll sit down howling !

---

* These verses lose much of their point in modern ears from being nothing if not personal. Ctesias, Prepis, Lysistratus, and Pauson are mere names to us ; Cleonymus has been mentioned before in this play as a gentleman of capacious dimensions, and we gather elsewhere that he was a coward and a bully. Hyperbolus made a large fortune by selling lamps— and votes too, said his enemies ; but the former sin was more heinous to Aristophanes. After Cleon's death he became a second edition of that demagogue. The Cratinus here mentioned was not the great comic dramatist whose "Bottle" gained the first prize against Aristophanes' masterpiece, the "Clouds ;" but one of those mediocre poets whose existence is proverbially considered unnecessary by gods, men, and the columns of the Reviews.

And no one else in purchasing provisions shall bamboozle you!
Cleonymus shan't jostle you, nor filthy Prepis tousle you!
    A cloak you'll wear of virgin white
    No sycophant has brought to light;
        Nor shall Hyperbolus provoke you,—
        With suits to choke you.

Nor shall Cratinus hop to you, his morning jests to bandy,
Smooth-shaven with a single shear like any gay young dandy;
    That busy trifler with the Muse,
    That knave in Artemonian shoes *
        From whose rank armpits you may gather
        What goat's his father.

Pauson no more'll be scoffing, nor Lysistratus importunate;
That shame of the Cholargeans, that double-dyed unfortunate,
    Who begs and shivers every day,
    And every month is starved, they say,
        For all the thirty days, and dirty—
        For more than thirty!

Enter a Bœotian *and* Boy, *followed by many* Pipers, *playing.*

Bœotian. Be gorra! it's right shoulder-galled I was!
Put down the pennyroyal, Ismenias,—

---

* Artemon was an engineer of great skill and fame, who used to be carried to his work in a litter. He is said, I know not upon what authority, to have been lame, and the expression "an Artemon in a litter" became proverbial, possibly to denote any man of great skill in his profession. However, the epithet "in a litter," which reminds one of "Mæcenate supino," seems to point a further meaning. Whether Artemon's lameness was real or affected, he may, like many men of real industry and talent, have assumed an idle and careless manner. In that case the proverb would apply to a man who pretended to be more idle and empty-headed than he really was, and to term Cratinus "a knave in Artemonian shoes" would be like calling him a Lord Melbourne without the brains.

Nately, now nately—and those pipers round you
That followed us from Thabes——

    Enter DICÆOPOLIS.

 Dic.   Stop! Stop! Confound you!
You buzzing wasps! Be off! Go to perdition!
Was Chæris then your bumble-pipe musician? [*Exeunt* Pipers.
 Bœot. Now, faix, your honour, I'm obliged to ye,
It's all the way from Thabes they've followed me,
Puffing and blowing all my blossoms down!
Now, if ye plase, buy what I've brought to town;
I've got young chicks and every four-winged cratur!
 Dic. Well met, my little pumpernickel-eater!
How do you do, my tight little Bœotian?
What have you brought us with all this commotion?
 Bœot. The vera best intirely ye could find
In ould Bœotia. Mats of ivery kind,
Wicks, pennyroyal, woodcocks, jackdaws, ducks,
Divers and water-hens and hazel-chucks——
 Dic. You're like a winter gale, man, bringing fowls
To market in such flights!
 Bœot.   Faix, and I've owls,
Beavers, geese, hares, moles, foxes, cats, hedgehogs,
Otters and weasels, eels from Copæ's bogs——
 Dic. O food to mortal man the best and fairest!—
Let me address the eels if such thou bearest!
 Bœot. "First-born of fifty virgins!"—Copaids!
Turn out, to plase his honour, when he bids!
 Dic. "O maiden of my love! O pined-for long!
Thou'rt welcome to the lords of comic song!"—
Beloved of Morychus!—Be quick, you fellows!
Bring me out here the gridiron and the bellows!—

"Behold her, swains, the loveliest eel and best!
After six years she seeks the yearning breast!
Speak to her, children"!—I'll supply the charcoal;—
"All for the potence of her sweet eyes' sparkle!"
Now bring her in. "Oh, may not Death's oppressing
Rob me of thee"—well-stewed with beet-root dressing!*

   Bœot. But how will I be paid for it, your honour?

   Dic. Oh!—as a market toll we'll look upon her!—
But will you sell me something else as well?
Eh? What d'ye say?

   Bœot.   There's nothing I won't sell!

   Dic. Come now, how much d'ye want for all the pack?
Or will you take another cargo back?

   Bœot. Just what you've got here and we go without.

   Dic. Ah! then you'll buy Phalerian sprats, no doubt,
Or crockery?

   Bœot.   What? Is it sprats or crockery?
We've got thim both at home. Nay, no such mockery!
I'll take what's common here, and what we want.

   Dic. I have it! Bring him out a sycophant!
And pack him up like crockery-ware.

   Bœot.   That's it!
By all the saints! it's a good sum I'd git,
Showing him as a tricksy queer baboon!

   Dic. Here comes Nicharchus, who'll denounce ye soon.

   Bœot. It's small he is.

   Dic.   But every inch is bad.

---

* These quotations are from the tragic poets, the last line being a parody upon Admetus' speech to his wife in the "Alcestis" of Euripides:

     "Oh, may not Death's oppressing
      Rob me of thee, my sole remaining blessing!"

Morychus was an epicure.

Enter NICHARCHUS, *an* Informer.

Nich. Whose wares are these?
Bœot. Sure, and they're mine, bedad,
From Thabes.
Nich. Then I denounce them, every one,
As goods of the enemy!
Bœot. What have they done,
The tiny birds, to make you storm and clatter?
Nich. And I'll denounce you too.
Bœot. Why, what's the matter?
Nich. I'll tell you, that the audience may know.
You've got a wick from the enemy in tow!
Dic. And so you're bringing now a wick to light!
Nich. Yes; it might burn the dockyard down, it might!
Dic. A wick a dockyard?
Nich. Yes.
Dic. But in what manner?
Nich. It might be stuck by some Bœotian planner (*looking hard at the* Bœotian)
Upon a kind of beetle, set alight
And sent into the dockyard some dark night
In a high wind, up through a water-drain.
And then the fire would catch the ships, it's plain,
And they'd all blaze at once!
Dic. (*belabouring him*). They'd blaze at once!
All through a beetle and a wick, you dunce!
Nich. I call you all to witness!
Dic. Gag him! Gag him!
Give me some straw to stuff him in, and bag him
Like crockery, that he mayn't break as we drag him!

Chorus. Now pack his purchase up, my man,
As tight and firmly as you can,
   Safe to make it,
Lest on the way he break it!
Dic. I'll see to that! He rings just like
(*Beating him*) A fire-cracked vessel when you strike,
   Jarring direly;—
An utter scamp entirely!
Chor. But what use will he be to him?
Dic. A jar to suit his every whim,
A bowl of abuses, a mortar of actions,
A lamp to throw light on official transactions,
A poisonous cup made to stir up
Plots and seditions and troublesome factions!
Chor. How could you trust a jar like this,
   That always gives so false a token?
Dic. Its strength, my friend, is not amiss:
   Hold it head-down, it can't be broken.
Chor. (*to* Bœotian).
   Now you're well off, my hearty!
Bœot. I'll join a reaping party!*
Chor. Ay, reap him down, my jolly clown,
And use him well, in field and town,
   For all you want;—
The perfect sycophant!

Dic. (*to audience*). I had hard work to pack that scoundrel there!

(*To* Bœotian) Here, my Bœotian, take your crockery ware!

Bœot. (*to* Boy). Come, get your shoulder under him, gossoon!

---

* The informer, packed in straw and tied at both ends, resembles a sheaf of wheat, and the Bœotian thinks his experience in this kind of work sufficient to enable him to do some real harvesting.

Dic. Be very careful how you hold the loon!
He's a very rotten burden, any way;
But still, be careful! If you get good pay,
And make some money by your importation,
You'll get some good out of an information!
        [*Exit* Bœotian *and* Boy.

    Enter LAMACHUS'S Slave.

 Slave. Ho! Dicæopolis!
 Dic.   Well, why d'ye shout?
 Slave. Why, Lamachus desires you'll send him out
Some thrushes for this drachma here, d'ye see?
And a Copaic eel for the other three!
 Dic. An eel for Lamachus! What Lamachus?
 Slave. The dauntless one, the "bull-hide-valorous," *
Who wields the Gorgon shield, and waves above
"Three overshadowing plumes."
 Dic.   Nay then, by Jove,
If he'd give me his shield, he shouldn't have the dish!
Let him wag his plumes over some salted fish!
If he makes any outcry or resistance,
I'll call the market stewards to my assistance!   [*Exit* Slave.
Now for my part I shall take up this load
And go back singing to my own abode.

(*Sings*) "'Quails and blackbirds!' fluttering spread
    Purple pinions o'er my head."
          [*Exit* DICÆOPOLIS.

---

 * This is an Homeric epithet of Ares, the meaning of which seems to be "valorous with a shield of bulls' hides," or "valorous against shields of bulls' hides."

*Chorus.**

STROPHE.

Thou hast seen him, O my city!
　　Thou hast seen the master mind!
So far-sighted, wise, and witty,
　　He alone a truce has signed!!
He alone at peace with Sparta,
Fearlessly can buy and barter
　　Merchandise of every kind!

Every blessing, every grace,
Flows upon his favoured race!
All the thrifty wife would choose
For her daily household use;
Every dainty steaming dish
That the starving soul could wish.
Never more will I admit
War beside my hearth to sit,
Never at my board shall he
Troll Harmodius's glee.†
Drunken fiend! whose revel riot
Burst upon our happy quiet,
Spoiling, ruining, destroying,
Blessings we were all enjoying.
Frenzied, insolent marauder!
None could win him back to order.
Though one spoke him soft and fair,

---

* The Chorus are now quite converted to the views of Aristophanes, and sing this *palinode*, expressive of their hatred for war and admiration of the wisdom of all peace-makers, and of Dicæopolis in particular.

† The well-known drinking-song beginning—

　　"I'll wreathe my sword with myrtle bough,
　　The sword that laid the tyrant low."

"Prithee, take a seat, good sir!
Taste this loving-cup, my friend!
Drink, and let all quarrels end!"
Still his wrath but raged the higher,
Till he set our poles on fire,
Till at last a blacker treason
   Seized him, and he drew our wine,
Stored and bottled for the season,
   From its skins—upon the vine!

Antistrophe.

He, departing in his glory,
   Goes the banquet to prepare!
Proudly, see! he casts before ye
   Tokens of his festal fare!
See! displayed before his dwelling
All those feathers, surely telling
   Of the princely dainties there!*

Come, thou nymph of jocund mien,
Playmate of the Cyprian queen!
Lovely Peace! whom none can ever
From the laughing Graces sever!
Wherefore didst thou hide from sight
Thy celestial visage bright?
Would some Cupid sly would tether
You and me, dear love, together,
All with twisted braids of roses,
And a hundred different posies,

---

* It was a peculiar vanity of the Athenians to hang up bunches of feathers outside their houses when any great entertainment was going forward within.

Like that wingèd Boy divine,
Limned in Aphrodite's shrine !*
Though perchance thou deemest me
All too old a groom for thee,
Three things I will do beside
When I bring thee home a bride.
First, I shall draw out in order
Rows of vines, and round the border
Set some fig-trees' tender shoots,
And the slips of wild-wood roots.
Then I'll plant in ordered rows
Olives round our orchard-close.
This I think to do, though laden
   With a weight of years, that we
May anoint us both, dear maiden,
   When the new-faced moon we see.

Enter DICÆOPOLIS, Herald, Slaves, *etc.*

Her. Hear, all ye people ! As our sires ordained,
At trumpet-call the gallons shall be drained ; †
The man who drains his gallon first to own
The drinking prize, the skin of—Ctesiphon.

Dic. Lads ! Women ! Don't ye hear ? What are you doing ?
Didn't you hear the herald ? To your stewing !
Roast ! Turn ! Weave chaplets ! and take off that hare !
Bring me the spits to spit those thrushes there !

---

* This alludes to the celebrated "Eros" of Zeuxis, which was in the temple of Aphrodite.

† A prize of a skin of wine was given on the second day of the festival Anthesteria, to the person who, at a certain bugle-call, should first swallow a gallon of wine—a feat which we shall find Dicæopolis achieves. To-day an extraordinary prize is offered, the largest skin procurable, which is that of the Daniel Lambert here mentioned.

Chor.   I envy your design so wise,
          Still more the feast you're making!
Dic.   And what then when you cast your eyes
          Upon these thrushes baking?
Chor.   There, too, you're right completely!
Dic.   Come, give the fire a poking!
Chor.   You see how very neatly
         How dinner-like and featly
          He manages his cooking!

Enter a Countryman.

Countryman. Oh dear! Oh dear!
Dic.   Good Lord! who's that just come!
Count. A miserable man!
Dic.   Then—go back home! *
Count. Kind sir, there's no one has a peace but you—
Measure me out at least a five-year brew!
Dic. What's come to you?
Count.   I've lost my beasts and all!
Dic. How?
Count.   The Bœotians stole them from their stall
At Phylæ.
Dic.   That's a blow that must have smarted!
But—why aren't you in black for the departed?
Count. Ay, though they always kept me well, I vow—
In good manure.
Dic.   Well, what do you want now?
Count. I've wept my eyes out for them beasts of mine!
Oh, if your kind heart does at all incline

---

* ".What are you? Are you merry? You must be very merry if you enter."—" The Knight of the Burning Pestle," Act v. scene 3.

To Derketes of Phylæ, then, I pray,
Anoint my eyes with peace, without delay.

Dic. I'm not the parish doctor, my poor chap.

Count. Come! come! I pray you, do! for then, mayhap,
I shall get back my oxen!

Dic.   Oh dear no!
Go and lament to Pittalus and Co!*

Count. Only a drop of peace! Just squeeze me one
Into this little tube.

Dic.   I'll give you none!
Not a bird's whistle! Off now, with your tears!

Count. Oh dear! oh dear! my poor dear farming steers!
                                [*Exit* Countryman.

Chor. Our friend seems to find the peace to his mind,
And to share it with any he seems disinclined!

Dic. Pour honey, there, over the tripe in that dish!
And mind how you're frying those fine cuttle-fish!

Chor.   Do you hear? What a bellow!

Dic.   The eels! Broil them there!

Chor.   Stop! Stop! my dear fellow!
           You'll kill us, I swear!
           Of hunger I'm dying,
              And the folk who live near,
              With the smell of good cheer
           And the noise of your crying!

Enter a Bridesman *and* Bridesmaid.

Dic. Now then, roast this, and brown it well with care!

Bridesman. Ho! Dicæopolis!

Dic.   Who's there? Who's there?

Brid. A bridegroom sends you from the wedding feast
This dish of meat.

---

* Pittalus was an Athenian doctor.

Dic. That's very kind at least,
Whoever he is.
Brid. And he desires you too
To pour out, in return for this same stew,
One cup of peace into this alabaster,
To keep him safe from service and disaster.
Dic. There—take your meat away! Don't give me any!
I wouldn't do it for a pretty penny!
But who's this girl? (*turning to the* Bridesmaid.)
Brid. The bridesmaid: she comes here
Sent by the bride to gain your private ear.
Dic. (*to* Bridesmaid). Come, then, my dear, what is it? (*The* Bridesmaid *whispers to him.*) Well, I'm blest!
What a ridiculous, absurd request!
She wants to keep her husband safe at home!
Well, bring the truces—I must give her some,
Since she's a woman and unfit for war.
So, girl, just reach me here that ointment jar :—
And tell the bride, whene'er they raise recruits,
To drop some grease into her husband's boots.
[*Exit* Bridesman *and* Bridesmaid.
Take back the truces. Bring that filter o' mine,
That I may fill the gallons up with wine.
Chor. Lo! here comes one with lifted brows and pale,
Speeding, like one that bears a woeful tale!

Enter a Messenger.

Mess. Oh, general grief, and grievous generals!

Enter LAMACHUS.

Lam. What voice re-echoes round the brass-girt halls?
Mess. The generals bid you hasten in full feather

To guard the passes in this snowy weather.
They've heard that the Bœotians will attack us
While we are busy with the feast of Bacchus.

Lam. Oh, generals, were your wisdom as your numbers!
Isn't it hard to rob me of my slumbers
Like this, and drag me from the feast Lenæan?

Dic. Ho! Armament Duello-Lamachæan!

Lam. Oh dear! and now thou'rt mocking me with jests!

Dic. Wouldest thou strive with Geryon's four—crests?*

Lam. Out, out, alas!
Ah! what a message did the herald bear me!

Dic. Ha! with what message does this herald near me!

Enter Messenger.

Mess. Ho! Dicæopolis!

Dic. Well, well; what is it?

Mess. The priest of Dionysus hopes you'll visit
The feast at once—with box and gallon too—
Quick! Raise the dust! The dinner's stayed for you
This long time—all the things are ready—benches,
Footstools and tables, cushions, chaplets, wenches,
Dried fruits and comfits, honey-cakes and myrrh,
Sesame-puddings, broad-cakes—all are there.
Be quick! Make haste! [*Exit* Messenger.

Lam. Oh dear! my evil fate!

Dic. Why, yes; you trust to the protectorate
Of a big Gorgon!—Shut the door, you sinner,
And let somebody be preparing dinner!

Lam. Ho! boy, there! Bring me out my haversack!

Dic. Ho! boy, there! Bring me out my box to pack!

* Dicæopolis probably here sticks four feathers in his hair, ridiculing the three plumes of Lamachus's helmet. Geryon was a mythological giant with three heads, six arms, six feet, and four wings.

Lam. Some salted thyme and onions, boy, be quick!
Dic. Some fish for me, boy: onions make me sick!
Lam. Boy, bring me out a mess of rotten fish!
Dic. And me a mess too—for a savoury dish.
Lam. Bring me the feather which my helmet brushes!
Dic. Bring me the pigeons and the little thrushes!
Lam. How fair and white is this tall ostrich crest!
Dic. How fair and brown is this roast pigeon's breast!
Lam. Sirrah! forbear to mock my martial arms!
Dic. Sirrah! forbear to eye my thrushes' charms!
Lam. Bring out the hair-trunk where my crest reposes!
Dic. Bring out the hare-stew that delights our noses!
Lam. This moth was eating up my tufts so shining!
Dic. This mouth is eating hare-soup before dining!
Lam. Don't worry me, sir, with your conversation!
Dic. No;—but this boy and I've a disputation.
(*To* Boy) Now, will you bet?—let the decision rest
With Lamachus—if locusts be the best—
Or thrushes.

Lam.   Bah! You're insolent!
Dic.   You hear it!
He said that locusts had the greater merit!*

Lam. Ho! boy, take down, and bring me out, my spear!
Dic. Ho! boy, take off the tripe and bring it here!
Lam. Come, I will draw my lance from forth its cover,
(*To* Boy) Stand fast, and pull.
Dic.   And you, boy, pull this over! †

---

* This was the last thing he would have said, thrushes being a delicacy, and the popular superstition about locusts being that those who lived upon them were eaten up in their old age by winged vermin bred in their insides (cf. "Laurembergii Horticultura Præloq." p. 9).

† As Lamachus is pulling his lance from its cover, Dicæopolis, with the aid of the boy, pulls the spit out of some roast joint.

Lam. Bring me the stand that holds my staff of strife!
Dic. Bring me the bread out, lad, my staff of life!
Lam. Bring me the oval Gorgon-compassed shield!
Dic. And me the pancake's cheese-encompassed field!
Lam. This insolence is broad! I'll none of it!
Dic. This broad-cake's good—I'll have another bit!
Lam. Boy, pour the oil out! In this bronze I see
An old man being tried for treachery!
Dic. Pour out the honey! Here's an old man's face
Who curses Lamachus's *Gorgon* race.
Lam. Bring me my breastplate, boy, my aid in war!
Dic. Bring me *my* breastplate, boy—my gallon jar!
Lam. Herewith I'll arm myself the foe to rout!
Dic. Herewith I'll arm me—for a drinking bout!
Lam. Boy, strap my bedding to the shield this minute!
Dic. Boy, strap the meat-box with my dinner in it!
Lam. Give me the knapsack—on my back I'll bear it!
Dic. Give me the cloak; upon my way I'll wear it!
Lam. Take up the shield, boy, and we'll quit this folly!
It's snowing! Ugh! Things look most melancholy! [*Exit.*
Dic. Take up the dinner; things look very jolly! [*Exit.*

Chorus.

See the twain to battle sped.
But what diverse ways they tread!
One will sit and feast all night
With a wreath of roses dight
    Drinking hard;
While the other sits and shivers
With a thousand quakes and quivers,
    Keeping guard!

Strophe.

May that scion of slobber, that quill-driving jobber,
   Antimachus, scribbler of verse,*
Without reservation or equivocation
   Be—damned with the Thunderer's curse!
For, when president o'er us, as head of the Chorus
   On Bacchus's festival day,
The miserly beast shut me out from the feast,
   And sent me quite famished away!
May I see him half-dying for cuttle-fish frying!
   When bubbling, and hissing, and nice,
With salt ready stored it hangs o'er the board,†
   And lands on his plate in a trice;
Then, just ere he slips the first slice in his lips
   May a little dog steal through the door,
Make a snatch at the dish, run away with the fish,
   And never be found any more!

Antistrophe.

One plague we have reckoned. And now may a second
   Befall him as well—in the night—
Going home from a ride with a pain in his side,
   In a feverish pitiful plight;
Ere he reach his abode may some Knight of the Road,
   Of wassail and insolence full—
Orestes pursued by the Furies ‡—intrude
   Upon him, and batter his skull!

---

* Antimachus was nicknamed "son of slobber" from his unpleasant habit of spluttering. He was "choregus" at the time when Aristophanes' "Banqueters" was produced, and did not invite the poet to the entertainment which he then gave the chorus.

† *i.e.* the table, with a play upon *sea*-board.

‡ Orestes was a notorious footpad of the day. He is humorously confused with his great namesake, the son and murderer of Clytemnestra.

In a terrible taking while cut-purse is breaking
   His head may he look all around,
And grope in the dark, very wide of the mark,
   To pick up a stone from the ground;
And finding at last a missile to cast—
   No matter what— not what he seeks—
Take aim as he can—and, missing his man,
   Bespatter Cratinus's cheeks!

Enter a Messenger.

Mess. Ye slaves that dwell in Lamachus's mansion! *
Water! heat water in a little panshin!
Make ready linen, greasèd wool, and plaster
To bandage up the ankle of your master!
The man was wounded, leaping o'er a trench
Upon a treacherous stake; the backward wrench
Unhinged his ankle, and, with awful shock,
He burst his head flat fallen upon a rock!
Started the Gorgon from her case of leather,
And down the cliff was hurled the Boaster's feather.
Loud rang the death-cry of the hapless wight;—
"Farewell, great orb; I leave thy glorious light,†
To see it never more! I die a martyr!"
So spake and straightway fell into the water.
Rose up, and found some base deserters near,
And routed all the robbers with his spear.
But throw the doors apart—for he is here!

   * This speech is a parody upon the narratives of "messengers" in the tragedians, as the subsequent lamentations of Lamachus are upon the groanings of tragic heroes.
   † He addresses his shield in the terms in which the heroes of tragedy bid farewell to the sun.

Enter LAMACHUS, *wounded, supported by two* Slaves.

Lam.   Woe, woe, unutterable woe!
        Oh, icy pang! Oh dear!
     Alack! I go to realms below
        From wound of foeman's spear.
     But 'twere indeed a grievous shock
        If Dicæopolis
     Should see me wounded here, and mock
        Such woeful fate as this!

Enter DICÆOPOLIS, *drunk, supported by two* Dancing-girls.

Dic.   Ho! ho! Unutterable bliss!
        My golden chicks, I thirst
     For one soft kiss! What joy is this!
        I've drunk the gallon first!
Lam.   O wretched state!
        O woeful fate!
     Alack! Alack! Alack!
        My horrid wounds would shock ye!
Dic.   Ho! Lamachus, come back!
        How do, my little jockey?
Lam.   Foul hate is mine!
Dic.   I've no repose!
Lam.   Don't kiss me, swine!
Dic.   Don't bite my nose!
Lam. Oh dear! what damages! That charge was heavy!
Dic. What *charge* to-day could anybody levy? *
Lam. Apollo! Healer! Unto thee I call!

   * On festivals the ordinary club-dinners, for which the members were charged so much a head, did not take place, but were superseded by such entertainments as that from which Dicæopolis has just returned.

Dic. It isn't now the Healer's festival!

Lam. Convey me instant, on a healing mission,
To Pittalus, the eminent physician!

Dic. And bear me away,
To the Judges, I pray.
Is the King * within?
Then give me the skin!

Lam. A cruel spear has pierced my bones in horrid gruesome fray!

Dic. There! look at that! I've emptied it! Hurrah! I've won the day!

Chor. Sing ho! Sing ho! the conqueror! You bid us all sing Hollo!

Dic. Yes, and I filled one full of wine and drank it at a swallow!

Chor. Bravo! Hurrah! my noble heart! The skin is yours! Hurray!

Dic. Then follow me, and sing Hurrah! Bravo! He's won the day!

Chorus. We'll fill your train,
As you go in,
And cheer again,
You and your skin,
With a hearty strain—
He's won the day!
With a hip-hip-hip-hurray!

---

* The Archon who presided at the Lenæan festival, and who would present him with the prize.

CPSIA information can be obtained
at www.ICGtesting.com
Printed in the USA
LVHW081417160919
631218LV00018B/857/P

9 781356 525928